Instruments and Music

Keyboards

Daniel Nunn

www.raintreepublishers.co.uk
Visit our website to find out
more information about
Raintree books.

To order:

☎ Phone 0845 6044371
▤ Fax +44 (0) 1865 312263
▤ Email myorders@raintreepublishers.co.uk

Customers from outside the UK please telephone +44 1865 312262

Raintree is an imprint of Capstone Global Library Limited,
a company incorporated in England and Wales having its
registered office at 7 Pilgrim Street, London, EC4V 6LB
– Registered company number: 6695582

Text © Capstone Global Library Limited 2012
First published in hardback in 2012
The moral rights of the proprietor have been asserted.

Edited by Dan Nunn, Rebecca Rissman, and Sian Smith
Designed by Joanna Hinton-Malivoire
Picture research by Mica Brancic
Production by Victoria Fitzgerald
Originated by Capstone Global Library Ltd
Printed and bound in China by Leo Paper Products Ltd

ISBN 978 1 406 22435 1 (hardback)
15 14 13 12 11
10 9 8 7 6 5 4 3 2 1

British Library Cataloguing in Publication Data
Nunn, Daniel.
   Keyboards. -- (Instruments and music)
   1. Keyboard instruments--Juvenile literature.
   I. Title II. Series
   786.1'9-dc22

Acknowledgements
We would like to thank the following for permission to reproduce
photographs: Alamy p **12** (© David Bartlett); Corbis p **17** (© Rick
D'Elia); Getty Images pp **11** (Taxi/Julie Toy), **14** (Redferns/Ebet
Roberts), **16** (Joey Foley), **18** (Datacraft/Hana), **20** (WireImage/
Shirlaine Forrest), **22** (AFP Photo/Yoshikazu Tsuno); iStockphoto.
com p **5** (© Jon Helgason); Photolibrary pp **4** (Stockbroker/Monkey
Business Images Ltd), **10** (Flirt Collection/Lawrence Manning), **13**
(imagebroker.net/Foto Beck), **15** (imagebroker.net/Egon Bömsch),
21 (Goodshoot), **23 bottom** (imagebroker.net/Egon Bömsch); Rex
Features p **19** (Evening Standard/Alex Lentati); Shutterstock pp **6**
(© Netfalls), **7 top left** (© Luchschen), **7 top right** and **23 top**
(© Nikita Rogul), **7 bottom right** (© Sbarabu), **7 bottom left** (©
Objectsforall), **8** (© Monkey Business Images), **9** (© Katrina Leigh).

Cover photograph of Flogging Molly in concert, New York, USA, 28th
Feb, 2008, reproduced with permission of Rex Features (Startraks/Matt
Hensley). Back cover photograph of a piano being played reproduced
with permission of Shutterstock (© Netfalls).

We would like to thank Jenny Johnson, Nancy Harris, Dee Reid, and
Diana Bentley for their assistance in the preparation of this book.

Every effort has been made to contact copyright holders of
material reproduced in this book. Any omissions will be rectified in
subsequent printings if notice is given to the publisher.

Contents

Keyboard instruments

piano

maraca

People play many instruments to make music.

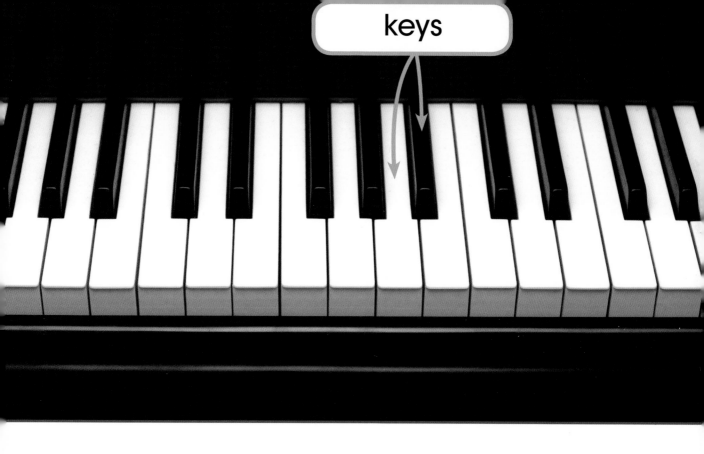

keys

A keyboard instrument has many keys to press.

People play notes by pressing different keys.

There are many kinds of keyboards.

Pianos

A piano is a keyboard instrument.

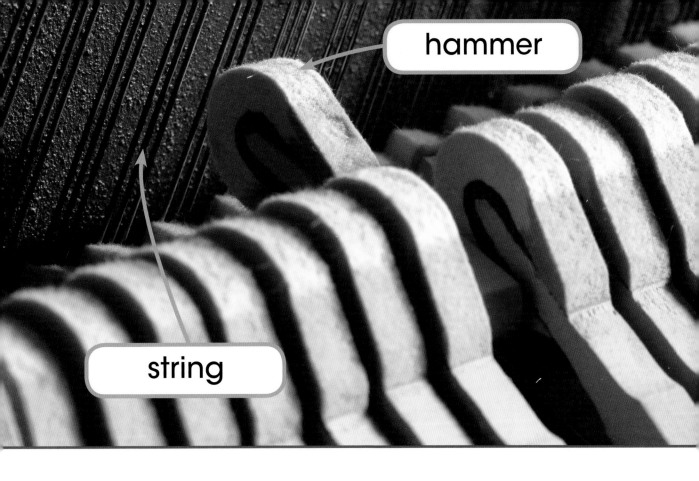

hammer

string

Pressing each key makes a hammer
hit a string inside the piano.

A grand piano is very big.

Other pianos are smaller.

Organs

An organ is a keyboard instrument.

pipe

A cathedral pipe organ is very big.

An electronic organ is smaller.

An accordion is an organ, too.
You squeeze it to make a noise.

Unusual keyboard instruments

A keytar is a keyboard you can carry with you.

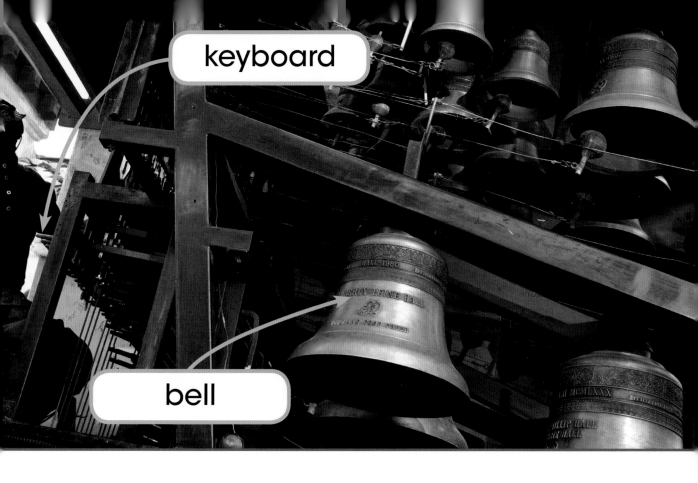

keyboard

bell

A carillon is a keyboard used to play
bells. It can play many bells at once.

Some people use computers to make music.

Some people use mobile phones to make music!

Playing keyboard instruments

Some people play keyboards
for work.

Some people play keyboards just for fun!

World's smallest grand piano?

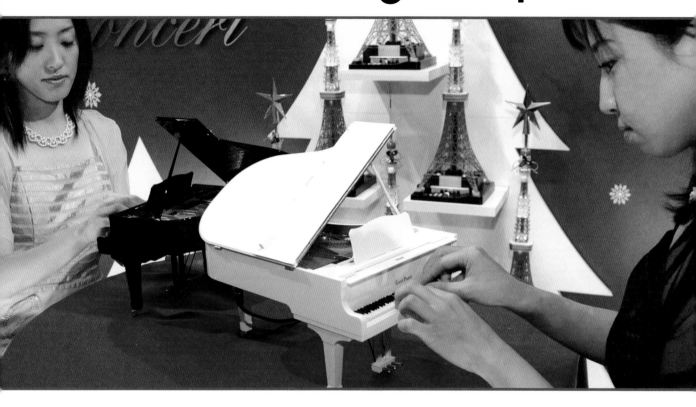

Could this be the smallest grand piano? It is not much bigger than

a hand!

Picture glossary

 **keyboard** set of keys arranged in two rows. People press keys to play notes.

 **note** sound made by a musical instrument

Index

Notes for parents and teachers
Before reading
If possible take the children somewhere where they can see a piano and hear it being played or use an electric keyboard. Explain that a keyboard is a set of keys arranged in rows. Sound is made when the keys are pressed. Press a key and ask the children if they think a high note or a low note is being played. Select children to press keys and repeat.

After reading
Make a really big keyboard instrument by giving eight children eight different chime bars from low c to high c. Ask another child to stand in front of them and when the child points at them, they have to play!

Extra information
Note for page 7: The instruments shown are: organ (top left), electric keyboard (top right), accordion (bottom left), and piano (bottom right).
Keyboards are not actually a category of musical instruments in themselves; instruments fall into the string, woodwind, brass, or percussion families. The harpsichord is a string instrument because its strings are plucked when the keys are pressed. The pipe organ makes its sound from air vibrating in a set of pipes. The pipes have reeds inside them. This makes it a woodwind instrument.